# The Story of Flight

# SPACE FLIGHT

# Crabtree Publishing Company
### www.crabtreebooks.com

PMB 16A, 350 Fifth Avenue,
Suite 3308
New York, NY 10118

612 Welland Avenue
St. Catharines, Ontario
L2M 5V6

**Published in 2004 by
Crabtree Publishing Company**

**Coordinating editor:** Ellen Rodger
**Project editors:** Sean Charlebois, Carrie Gleason
**Production coordinator:** Rose Gowsell

Created and Produced by
**David West 𐅨 Children's Books**

**Project Development, Design, and Concept**
David West Children's Books:
**Designer:** David West
**Editor:** Gail Bushnell
**Illustrators:** Terry Pastor, Gary Slater & Steve Weston
(Specs Art), James Field & Stephen Sweet (SGA),
Alex Pang
**Picture Research:** Carlotta Cooper

**Photo Credits:**
Abbreviations: t-top, m-middle, b-bottom, r-right,
l-left, c-center.

Front cover & pages 9t, 11 both, 12, 13, 14 both,
18t & bl, 20, 21t, 22, 23, 29t & br - NASA. 4, 5 -
The Culture Archive. 7, 9b, 17, 18br, 21b, 26 -
Corbis Images. 8 both - Rex Features. 16 - Katz
Pictures. 19 - Dr. Vadim P. Lukashevich. 25 -
Photo/Model: Eliot R. Brown.

06 05 04 03
10 9 8 7 6 5 4 3 2 1

**Library of Congress Cataloging-in-Publication Data**
Hansen, Ole Steen.
   Space flight / written by Ole Steen Hansen.
      p. cm. -- (The story of flight)
Includes index.
Contents: Into orbit -- First into space -- Fly me to the moon --
Moon walkers -- Lifting bodies & X-planes -- Space Shuttle 1 -- Space
Shuttle 2 -- Space Stations -- ISS -- Skimming space -- Space probes --
Mars exploration -- Spotters' guide..
ISBN 0-7787-1207-9 (RLB : alk. paper) -- ISBN 0-7787-1223-0 (PB :
alk. paper) 1432065
   1. Astronautics--Juvenile literature. 2. Space flight--History--
Juvenile literature. [1. Astronautics. 2. Space flight--History.] I. Title.
II. Series.
   TL793.H343 2003
   629.4'1--dc22
                                                    2003016002

# The Story of Flight

# SPACE FLIGHT

## Ole Steen Hansen

Crabtree Publishing Company
www.crabtreebooks.com

# CONTENTS

6 INTO ORBIT

8 FIRST INTO SPACE

10 FLY ME TO THE MOON

12 MOON WALKERS

14 LIFTING BODIES & X-PLANES

16 SPACE SHUTTLE 1

18 SPACE SHUTTLE 2

20 SPACE STATIONS

22 ISS

24 SKIMMING SPACE

26 SPACE PROBES

28 MARS EXPLORATION

30 SPOTTERS' GUIDE

32 INDEX AND GLOSSARY

**JULES VERNE**
In the 19th century, writer Jules Verne imagined sending people to the Moon by using a gun to launch the spacecraft.

# INTRODUCTION

**I**n 1969, the first astronauts walked on the Moon. It was only 66 years after the Wright brothers flew short hops in the first powered aircraft, and just eight years after the first human flew in space. Developments in space flight have moved extremely fast, but space is a harsh and unfriendly environment and it takes great courage to venture out into it.

## GODDARD

In 1926 Robert Goddard launched the world's first liquid fuel rocket. In this rocket, the fuels are in liquid form and not mixed until fired.

## V2 ROCKETS

Germany built V2 rocket powered missiles during World War II to bomb the cities of Europe. After the war, the scientists and engineers who helped to develop the missiles joined the U.S. and Russia in building rockets for space programs.

# INTO ORBIT

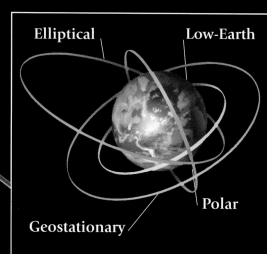

Elliptical      Low-Earth

Geostationary      Polar

## ORBITS

There are several different kinds of orbits. An elliptical orbit is one that is shaped like an elongated circle. When a satellite passes over or close to the Earth's poles, it is called a polar orbit. Space shuttles, space stations, and many satellites use a low-Earth orbit, which means that they are only 137 miles (220 km) above Earth's surface. Geostationary orbits occur 22,296 miles (35,880 km) above Earth. A satellite in geostationary orbit appears to remain in the same place in the sky because it circles Earth at the same speed as Earth rotates.

A satellite is a man-made object that is launched into space. Satellites orbit, or go around, Earth because of the pull of Earth's gravity.

For a satellite to escape the force of Earth's gravity and get into space, it must reach a speed of 24,856 mph (40,000 km/h). Satellites in low-Earth orbit are still pulled by gravity and need to fire small rocket engines to keep themselves in space. Satellites in geostationary orbit must achieve a careful balance between the pull of Earth's gravity and their speed. Effects from **solar wind** and other forces, such as **radiation**, mean that they must use small rocket **thrusters** to maintain their orbit.

## SPUTNIK

Sputnik weighed 185 lbs (84 kg) and was 1 ft 11 in (58 cm) across. It flew in an elliptical orbit, which took it around Earth in 96 minutes.

Satellites have **solar panels** to provide them with power. On October 4, 1957 the Soviet Union surprised the world by sending the first satellite, called Sputnik, into orbit. It was launched from the huge space center at Baikonur in Kazakhstan. It transmitted beeping radio signals as it flew and had equipment to measure the **density** and temperature of its surroundings throughout its orbit.

## Launchers

Rockets are used to send satellites and space ships into orbit. Here a satellite has been mounted on to a rocket launcher ready for lift-off. Satellites are positioned a few days early so that final checks can be made. The satellite is linked, via the rocket, to the control room, so it can be monitored during the final countdown.

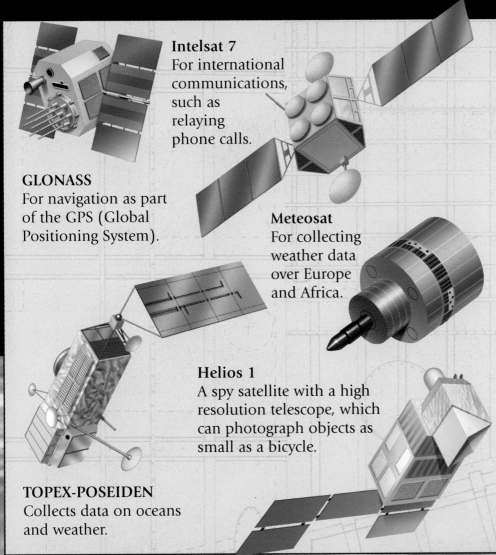

**Intelsat 7**
For international communications, such as relaying phone calls.

**GLONASS**
For navigation as part of the GPS (Global Positioning System).

**Meteosat**
For collecting weather data over Europe and Africa.

**Helios 1**
A spy satellite with a high resolution telescope, which can photograph objects as small as a bicycle.

**TOPEX-POSEIDEN**
Collects data on oceans and weather.

## TYPES OF SATELLITES

Some satellites, such as those used for spying, fly in low orbit about 217 miles (350 km) above Earth. Many other satellites fly in geostationary orbit above the equator, taking 24 hours to fly around the world. Geostationary satellites are used for internet connections, telecommunications, weather forecasts, and navigation. Thanks to these satellites it is easy and cheap to phone other continents. The world's first geostationary commercial communications satellite, the Intelsat Early Bird, was launched on April 6, 1965. **Meteorologists** also get precise information for their weather forecasts from geostationary satellites. Navigational satellites allow aircraft, ships, cars, and even explorers in the wilderness to use the Global Positioning System (GPS) to find out their position, with almost perfect accuracy.

# FIRST INTO SPACE

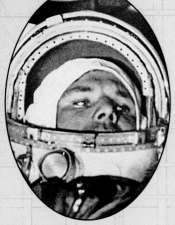

**YURI GAGARIN**
Gagarin was the first man in space. He was killed in 1968 in an airplane crash.

**T**he Sputnik flight began a space race between the United States and the Soviet Union. Both countries developed space programs, but it was the Soviet Union that put the first person in space.

Russian **cosmonaut** Yuri Gagarin traveled in space for 1 hour 48 minutes on April 12, 1961. Everything in the spacecraft was done automatically, so Gagarin was really the passenger on the trip. In earlier trips, a dog and various other animals had been sent into space. Going into space was dangerous. Laika, the Soviet space dog, died in 1957 when its spacecraft overheated on re-entering the **atmosphere**. Gagarin survived re-entry and was shot out of the spacecraft in his ejection seat, landing by parachute.

**VOSTOK 1**
Yuri Gagarin traveled in the Vostok 1 spacecraft. Gagarin sat in the round capsule at the top.

**VALENTINA TERESHKOVA**
In 1963, the Soviet cosmonaut Valentina Tereshkova, traveling in a Vostok 6, was the first woman in space and the tenth person to fly in orbit around Earth.

A-1 rocket

## JOHN GLENN

John Glenn orbited Earth three times on his 1962 space flight. He flew fighter planes in World War II before becoming an astronaut.

## MERCURY CAPSULE

The cramped one-man Mercury was the first manned U.S. spacecraft. Six manned flights were made between 1961 and 1963. The final one lasted 34 hours and 20 minutes, and 22 orbits were flown.

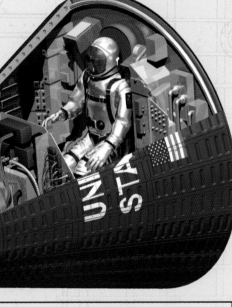

American astronauts did not like the idea of everything being automatic, so their spacecraft had more controls. In 1961, American astronauts made two flights, but not in full orbit. The first true American space flight was on February 20, 1962 by John Glenn. The first space walks, lasting 10 minutes, were carried out in 1965 by Soviet Lieutenant Colonel Alexei A. Leonov.

## SPACE WALKING

Astronauts "walking" in space travel around Earth just like a satellite in orbit. There is no oxygen in space and the temperature is a frigid -454°F (-270°C), so astronauts need to be well protected by their spacesuits. Over the years, spacesuits have been developed so they are more comfortable to wear and protect the astronaut from high levels of dangerous radiation from the Sun.

## ROCKETS

Both the Soviet Vostok and the U.S. Mercury were launched by rockets. Only rocket engines will work in space because there is no oxygen. Aircraft jet engines do not work, because they suck in oxygen and use it to burn fuel. Rockets carry their own oxygen, usually in liquid form. They also carry liquid fuel, usually hydrogen. Once the fuel and oxygen are pumped into the combustion chamber, an explosion occurs and the rocket is pushed forward.

Mercury-Atlas rocket

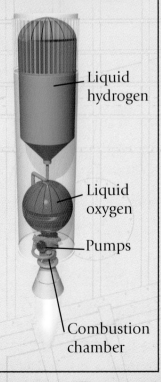

Liquid hydrogen

Liquid oxygen

Pumps

Combustion chamber

# FLY ME TO THE MOON

**MOON PROBES**
Soviet cosmonauts never landed on the Moon, but unmanned vehicles carried out research there. The Lunokhod 1 (below) conducted 500 soil tests.

The Soviets had many firsts during the early years of the space race. U.S. president John F. Kennedy announced in 1961 that the United States would land a man on the Moon and return him safely to Earth before the end of the decade.

This was the start of the Apollo program, one of the largest projects in history. New rockets and spacecraft were developed and tested, and astronauts were trained. In the 1960s the National Aeronautics and Space Administration (NASA) in the United States, employed 40,000 people while 350,000 additional people worked on the Apollo program in other ways. Thousands more worked on developing the computers and software necessary to make the technology work.

## A TRIP TO THE MOON

The Saturn V rocket sent the Apollo 11 spacecraft into Earth orbit (1). Two stages, or parts of the rocket, were **jettisoned** doing this and the third was discarded en route to the Moon (2). The Command and Service modules stayed in Moon orbit (3).

The Lunar module landed on the Moon (4). The top of the Lunar module then returned to Moon orbit and the two astronauts joined the third in the Apollo spacecraft (5). The Lunar module was then jettisoned and fell back to the Moon (6). The Command and Service modules left Moon orbit and separated near Earth (7). Finally, the Apollo Command module entered the Earth's atmosphere (8) and landed in the Pacific Ocean (9).

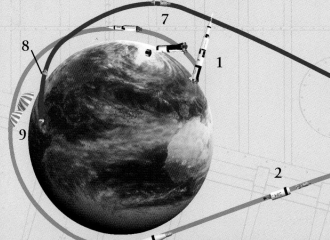

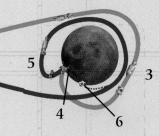

## SATURN V

The Apollo spacecraft was launched by the Saturn V rocket, which was 363 feet (110 m) tall. During the launch it used 40,000 gallons (150,000 liters) of fuel per minute.

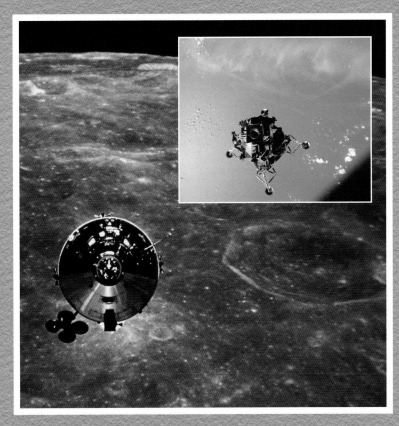

## SNOOPY AND CHARLIE BROWN GO TO THE MOON

The Apollo program progressed step-by-step with each spacecraft. The Apollo 7 in 1968 was the first manned Apollo flight, while Apollo 10, launched on May 18, 1969 was used as a dress rehearsal for Apollo 11's Moon landing. They even tested the Lunar module, nicknamed 'Snoopy,' meeting up with the Command and Service modules, nicknamed 'Charlie Brown.' Apollo 12, which landed on the Moon on November 19, 1969, was the first mission to set up major scientific experiments. The Apollo Moon astronauts are the only people to have seen the Moon up close.

The Moon is 238,617 miles (384,000 km) away. It takes light a little more than a second to travel that distance, while it would take a modern jet passenger aircraft eighteen days, if it was able to fly non-stop through space. The Apollo astronauts covered the distance in just three days.

# MOON WALKERS

**FIRST ON THE MOON**
(left to right) Neil Armstrong, commander and first man on the Moon, Michael Collins, who stayed in Moon orbit, and Buzz Aldrin, who was the second man on the Moon. Only 24 astronauts have traveled to the Moon. Twelve stayed in Moon orbit and twelve landed.

Apollo 11 was the first mission to land people on the Moon. During the mission, the automatic pilot failed and the astronauts had to maneuver the Lunar module over the edge of a moon crater to a safe landing site.

The landing burned up fuel and astronauts Neil Armstrong and Buzz Aldrin landed with nearly empty tanks. The control center in Houston, Texas noted that the astronauts had a heartbeat rate of 160 beats per minute, which is very high and shows that even astronauts get nervous in a dangerous situation! After six hours, the astronauts opened the hatch and went walking on the Moon. Their spacesuits weighed about 220 lbs (100 kg) on Earth, but only one sixth of the weight on the Moon, due to the lower gravity there.

## MOON LANDING AND TAKE-OFF

In Moon orbit two astronauts entered the Lunar module and descended to the Moon using a rocket engine to slow them down and land softly. The top part of the Lunar module was later used to leave the Moon and return to the Apollo Command and Service modules in Moon orbit. Leaving the Moon only took a small sized rocket engine, since the Moon's gravity is weak and there is no atmosphere.

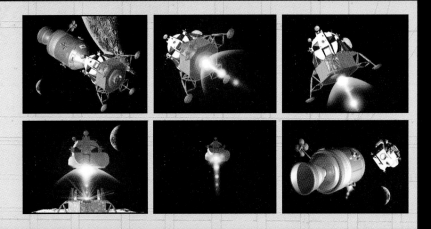

For two hours Armstrong and Aldrin carried out scientific work and set up the American flag. The astronauts then went back into the Lunar module, slept, and flew back into Moon orbit to join Collins the next day. When they returned to Earth in the Command module they parachuted into the Pacific Ocean. Back on Earth, the astronauts were checked over by doctors to make sure they were healthy.

### LUNAR ROVER

On later Apollo missions, an electrical Lunar Rover made it possible for astronauts to drive up to 6 miles (10 km) away from their landing sites to explore the surface.

### APOLLO 13

Apollo 13, launched on April 11, 1970, almost ended in disaster. On the way to the Moon an oxygen tank in the Service module exploded, leaving the astronauts short of oxygen and freezing cold in the damaged spacecraft. The astronauts had to use oxygen from the Lunar module and fly right around the Moon. It took them four days to get safely back to Earth.

# LIFTING BODIES & X-PLANES

The first flights by humans into space were made with rocket powered aircraft. These aircraft were research vehicles. They flew for only a few moments on the edge of space, yet they were necessary to explore the problems associated with high speed flight.

## X-PLANES

The American X-planes are research vehicles that have been used to test rockets, aircraft, and spacecraft. High speed flight, vertical take-off, unmanned flight, forward-swept wings, and flying on the edge of space have all been done by the X-planes. The first was X-1 (above left), which was the first aircraft to fly faster than the speed of sound.

The X-15 was the first U.S. test vehicle for space planes. It reached a height of 354,000 feet (107,899 m) and flew at Mach 6.7, or 6.7 times faster than the speed of sound. Overheating was a major problem on the X-15. The surface of the supersonic airliner, the Concorde, flying at Mach 2 reaches more than 212°F (100°C), but the X-15 had parts that were heated up to 1,832°F (1,000°C)!

## LIFTING BODIES

Most aircraft have wings for landing. In space flight, wings are not needed. Wings get in the way when entering Earth's atmosphere because they are heated up so much. Experiments have been carried out with "lifting body designs," which are vehicles that are able to fly without wings.

X-24A            M2-F3            HL-10

## X-15

The X-15 was launched from a B-52 bomber modified to carry it under its wing. While flying in Earth's atmosphere the X-15 was controlled like any other aircraft, but in space small rocket engines were used to change direction. After flying a few minutes, it glided down to Earth.

## PRINCIPLES OF LIFTING BODIES

On a lifting body aircraft, such as this X-24B, flown between 1973 and 1975, the fuselage, or body, is shaped like the wing of an aircraft. Air flowing over the top of the aircraft speeds up, creating **lift**. Experiments with lifting body designs have proved that an aircraft can actually fly without wings!

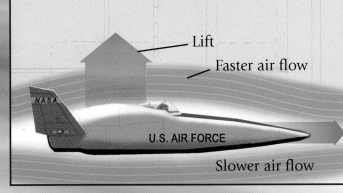

Lift

Faster air flow

Slower air flow

This meant that special metals to withstand heat had to be used on the aircraft. Three X-15s were built and 199 test flights were carried out between 1959 and 1968. The results from these supersonic test flights were useful in the design of the Space Shuttle. It was also important to find out the effects of space travel on the pilots. Special spacesuits were created, which were gradually developed into the spacesuits used for astronauts traveling to the Moon.

# SPACE SHUTTLE 1

A Space Shuttle lift-off is an impressive sight. With a weight equal to five Boeing 747 Jumbo jets, it takes a Shuttle just a few minutes to reach a speed of 17,399 mph (28,000 km/h), leave Earth's atmosphere, and enter orbit.

The Apollo Moon landings were very successful, but costly because a new spacecraft had to be built for each mission. In the 1970s, the United States wanted to create a cheaper space vehicle that could be reused on different missions.

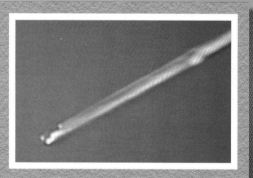

### IS IT SAFE?
Unfortunately, two Space Shuttles have been lost in accidents. The Challenger exploded in 1986 because of a leak in the booster rocket. Everyone on board was killed. In 2003, the Columbia burned up on re-entry into the atmosphere, just minutes before landing. This is a high number of accidents when compared to the number of flights made. Space travel is still far from being the safe everyday transport that airline flying has become.

### SPACE SHUTTLE BLAST-OFF
The astronauts are subjected to a 3G acceleration when the Shuttle is launched, which means that they feel three times more gravitational pull than normal. Every second 1,321 gallons (5,000 liters) of fuel is burned and exhaust gases reach a temperature of 5,792°F (3,200°C), which is hot enough to make iron evaporate!

One of the main problems in developing the Space Shuttle was finding a way to send as much fuel as the large spacecraft needed into space. Scientists solved the problem by positioning big fuel tanks and booster rockets outside the Shuttle. This way, the fuel tanks and booster rockets can be jettisoned several minutes after launch. The booster rockets attached to parachutes fall to Earth's surface and are reused, while the main fuel tank, which costs about 43 million dollars, breaks up when falling into the ocean. Six Space Shuttles have been built on this model. Since the first Space Shuttle launch in 1981 there have been over 100 missions.

## LANDING

The Space Shuttle needs a 2.8 mile-(4.5 km-) long runway to land. For re-entering the Earth's atmosphere the Shuttle is protected by heat resistant tiles, which can reach temperatures of up to 2,732°F (1,500°C) without melting.

## SPACE SHUTTLE ORBITER

The Shuttle Orbiter looks like a large airplane. The cargo bay is 60 feet (18.3 m) long and 15 feet (4.6 m) wide, and holds the equipment being put into space.

The ability to carry cargo into space has made Orbiter a very useful spacecraft. In space the Orbiter is powered by two engines and 44 small boosters.

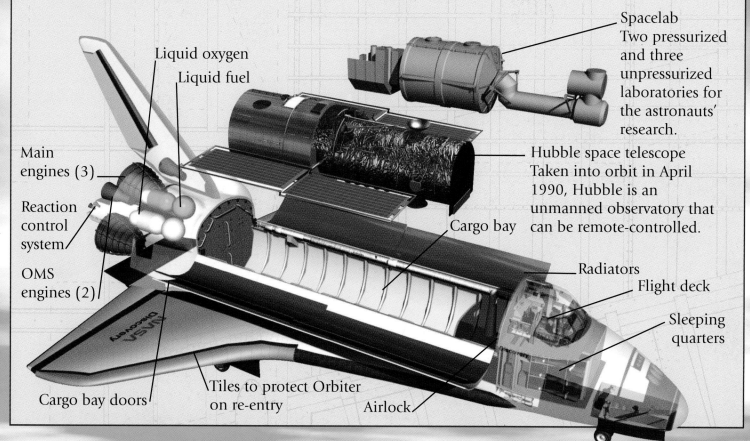

Liquid oxygen

Liquid fuel

Main engines (3)

Reaction control system

OMS engines (2)

Cargo bay doors

Tiles to protect Orbiter on re-entry

Airlock

Spacelab
Two pressurized and three unpressurized laboratories for the astronauts' research.

Hubble space telescope
Taken into orbit in April 1990, Hubble is an unmanned observatory that can be remote-controlled.

Cargo bay

Radiators

Flight deck

Sleeping quarters

# SPACE SHUTTLE 2

A Space Shuttle orbits the Earth in 90 minutes. Night and day change quickly when the astronauts fly at 217 miles (350 km) above Earth. Even though they travel at 17,400 mph (28,000 km/h), no motion is felt.

**THE FLIGHT DECK**
The Shuttle Flight deck has the same flight instruments and computer screens found in modern airliners and military aircraft. The cockpit has been improved since its design in the 1970s.

The Space Shuttle has made it possible for people who are not trained as astronauts, such as scientists, to work in space. When leaving the crew compartments to work outside, the crew are tethered, or connected by ropes, to the shuttle so they do not drift away. A lot of highly specialized technology was needed for the Space Shuttle, so it did not end up being a cheap, re-usable spacecraft. It was hoped that each flight would cost 100 million dollars, but the price turned out to be 500 million dollars.

**ENJOY YOUR MEAL**
On Shuttle missions the crew live in a weightless environment. When eating, a tray containing food is fastened down to stop it from drifting away. Moist foods cling to a spoon, so they are the best menu choice.

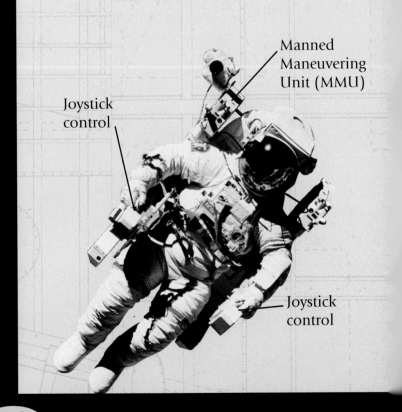

**MANNED MANEUVERING UNIT**
The manned maneuvering unit (MMU) was used by Shuttle crews in the mid 1980s. Once strapped into the MMU, it acted like a mini, one person spacecraft. The joystick controls were placed on the extended arms.

Manned Maneuvering Unit (MMU)

Joystick control

Joystick control

This is partly because it takes 25,000 people to make each Shuttle program successful. It also takes 17,000 work hours just to check and replace the 22,000 tiles that protect the Shuttle on re-entry.

## MISSION IN SPACE

Space Shuttle crew members are helping build the International Space Station (ISS). They also help service the Hubble Space Telescope, which makes it possible for **astronomers** to get much clearer images of space.

### BURAN

During the Cold War, the Soviet Union thought the U.S. Space Shuttle was a nuclear bomber. A Soviet space shuttle, called the Buran, was developed in response. The two shuttles look very similar in size and shape, but the Buran's powerful launch rocket means that it can lift more than a 100 ton load into space, which is more than the U.S. Shuttle. The Buran program was cancelled when it ran out of money, but there have been plans to resurrect it because of its high **payload**.

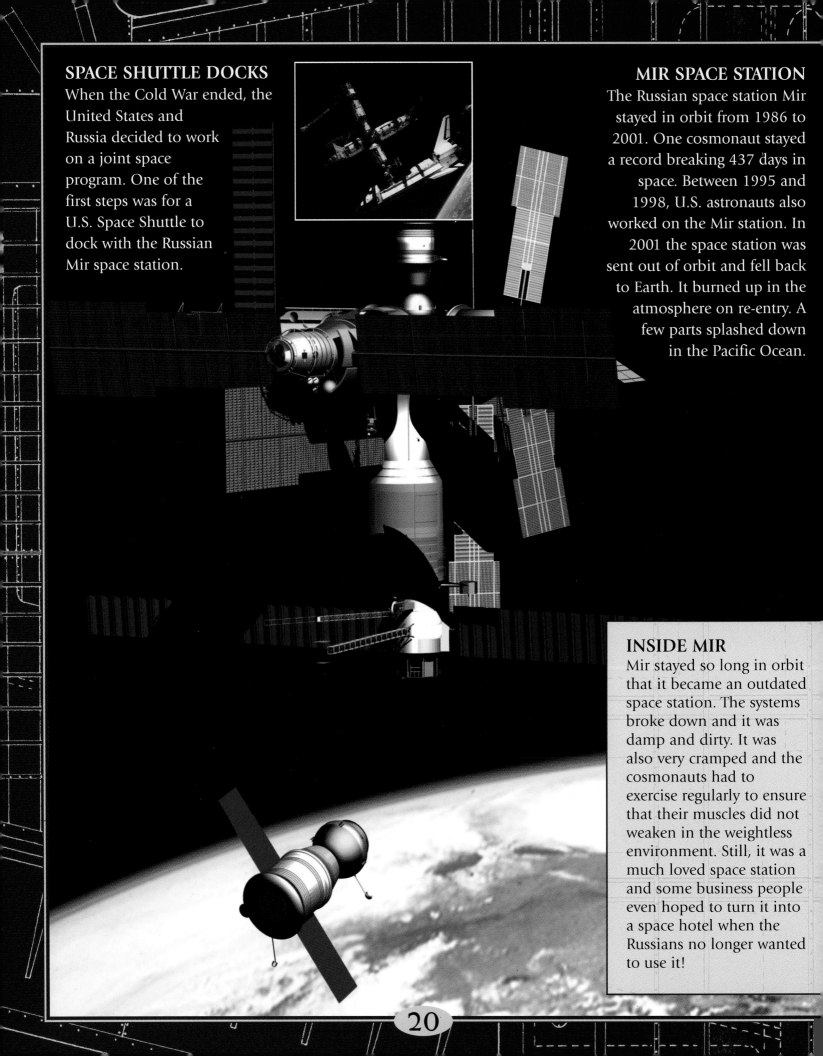

## SPACE SHUTTLE DOCKS

When the Cold War ended, the United States and Russia decided to work on a joint space program. One of the first steps was for a U.S. Space Shuttle to dock with the Russian Mir space station.

## MIR SPACE STATION

The Russian space station Mir stayed in orbit from 1986 to 2001. One cosmonaut stayed a record breaking 437 days in space. Between 1995 and 1998, U.S. astronauts also worked on the Mir station. In 2001 the space station was sent out of orbit and fell back to Earth. It burned up in the atmosphere on re-entry. A few parts splashed down in the Pacific Ocean.

## INSIDE MIR

Mir stayed so long in orbit that it became an outdated space station. The systems broke down and it was damp and dirty. It was also very cramped and the cosmonauts had to exercise regularly to ensure that their muscles did not weaken in the weightless environment. Still, it was a much loved space station and some business people even hoped to turn it into a space hotel when the Russians no longer wanted to use it!

# SPACE STATIONS

The Russians were beaten in the race to land people on the Moon, but their space stations have become one of the most important contributions to space exploration.

Space stations are craft which allow people to live in **pressurized**, oxygen-filled areas while in space, doing their research. On April 19, 1971, Salyut 1, the first spacecraft equipped as a space station, was sent into orbit. The U.S. Skylab followed in 1973. The Russian Mir space station stayed in orbit longer than any other. All these space stations flew in low-Earth orbit about 248 miles (400 km) above the surface. At this altitude the space stations have to be regularly boosted up into higher orbit to avoid falling back down to Earth.

## SALYUT
Salyut 1 carried scientific instruments that the crew used for observations. Unfortunately, the crew did not survive the trip, because Salyut leaked and the air left their spacecraft. The men on board were the first to die in space. Later Salyuts, like Salyut 3 (above) functioned better.

## SKYLAB
Skylab, the first U.S. space station, was built using the third stage from a Saturn V rocket left over from the Apollo program. Skylab stayed in orbit for six years. Much research was done from this roomy space station by three groups of astronauts. Some studies focused on the effect of long stays in the weightless conditions of space. Earth's environment was also observed.

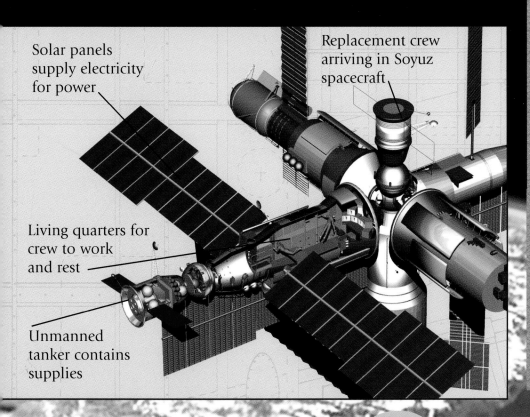

Solar panels supply electricity for power

Replacement crew arriving in Soyuz spacecraft

Living quarters for crew to work and rest

Unmanned tanker contains supplies

# ISS

The International Space Station (ISS) will be built by 2006, if the project is not delayed. ISS will be the biggest craft ever to orbit Earth. Astronauts will have a living and working space equal in size to a Boeing 747.

ISS is a special project not just because of its size, but also because it unites many countries for the first time. The United States, Russia, Canada, Japan, France, Brazil, and the United Kingdom are all involved. Joining forces allows the high cost of space projects to be shared. Parts used in space stations need to be of very high quality because in space it is even more difficult to repair and replace broken parts. Some people think that ISS is too expensive and should be scrapped. Others want to maintain a human presence in space, as a step toward distant goals such as landing on Mars.

**WHICH WAY UP**
Astronauts float around freely in the weightless conditions of the ISS. Astronauts train for this in water tanks. These tanks are especially useful for training astronauts who need to assemble parts of the station.

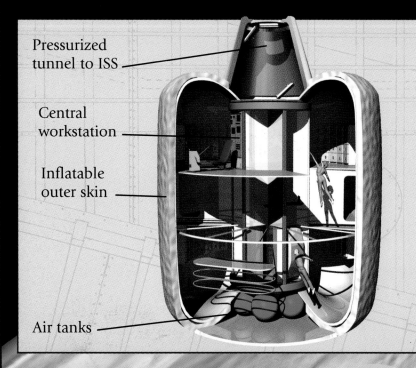

Pressurized tunnel to ISS

Central workstation

Inflatable outer skin

Air tanks

**INFLATABLE TRANSHAB MODULE**
It is costly to bring modules up for the ISS. A Shuttle flight can lift 20 tons into orbit at a cost of $500 million dollars. The Transhab Module is a plan to build an inflatable module for the ISS. It will be built from lightweight carbon fiber, which is the same material used to make bullet proof vests. It will take up little space during launch, but when inflated in orbit it will be strong enough to withstand the impact from the tiny **meteors** that will hit it. It might even be useful on future journeys to Mars, where saving weight and room on the spacecraft will be even more important.

Another idea for the future is space tourism. Two tourists have already visited the ISS even though it is not complete. The trip costs $20 million dollars and tourists have to undergo special training. Space experts think that orbiting hotels may be possible in 20 years.

## ISS

The ISS is built from over 100 separate modules and its total weight will be 448 tons. Eight pairs of solar panels will provide energy to run the space station.

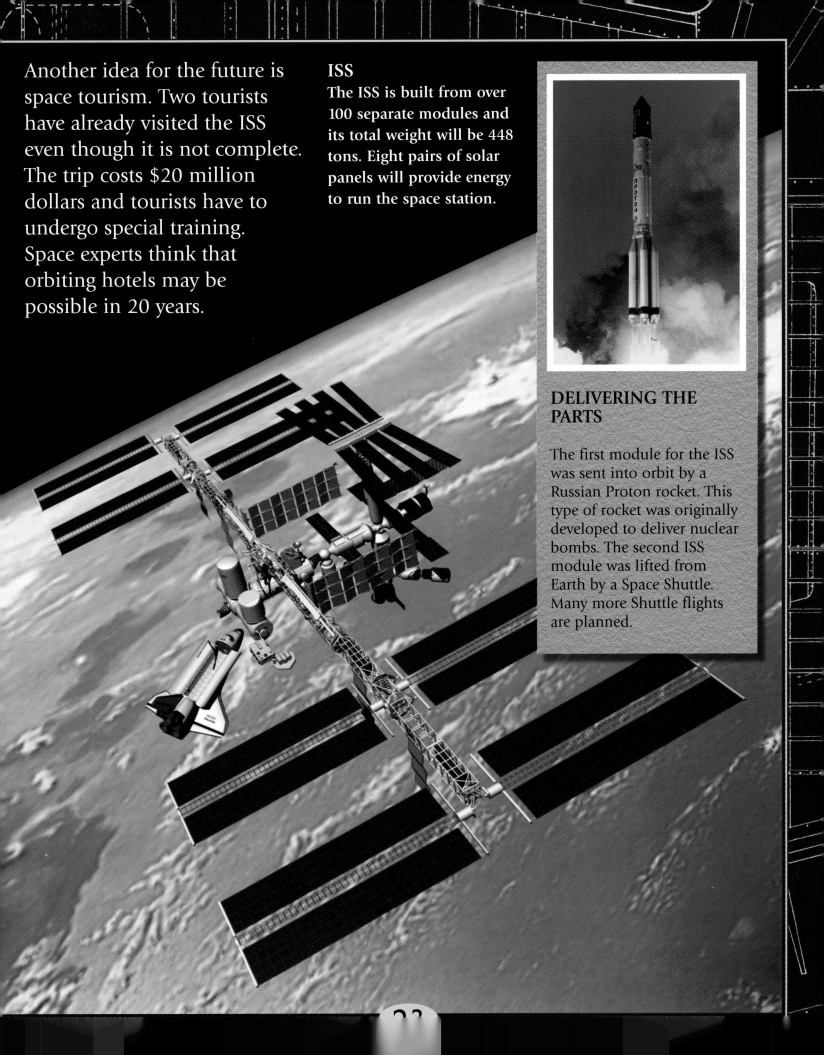

## DELIVERING THE PARTS

The first module for the ISS was sent into orbit by a Russian Proton rocket. This type of rocket was originally developed to deliver nuclear bombs. The second ISS module was lifted from Earth by a Space Shuttle. Many more Shuttle flights are planned.

# SKIMMING SPACE

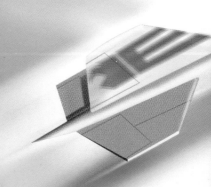

**T**oday, only a little more than 400 men and women have flown in space, the majority in low orbit. Most have been professional astronauts, some have been scientists, while two, so far, have been tourists on expensive tours of a lifetime!

**X-43B**
The X-43B is part of NASA's research program into hypersonic flight. The X-43B research vehicle is a step toward the development of airliners that fly at Mach 5, or five times the speed of sound, on the edge of space.

In the future, many more people may fly in space, especially if airliners designed to fly on the edge of space are built. The Concorde was fast and a fantastic technical success, but a newer, better one was never built. A new version would need to have a longer **range** and be able to seat more people to lower the ticket price. In order for it to be faster, it would have to be hypersonic.

## SCRAMJET

Hypersonic aircraft flying high in the thin atmosphere may use a scramjet engine. A scramjet engine has a core that is an ordinary jet engine for use at lower altitudes, where air is sucked in, compressed, and burned with fuel. When higher speeds and altitudes are reached and there is less air, this engine is cut off. Shutters force the air into the scramjet part where air is pressed into the combustion chamber by the high forward speed of the aircraft. The air is then burned with fuel and the aircraft is pushed along at high speed.

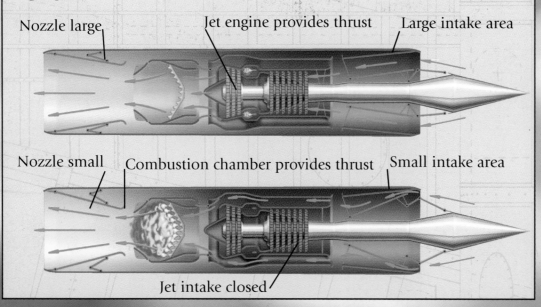

Nozzle large · Jet engine provides thrust · Large intake area

Nozzle small · Combustion chamber provides thrust · Small intake area

Jet intake closed

This means that it travels at five times the speed of sound or faster. It would need to be built from highly heat resistant metals. It would also need to travel in space to minimize **drag**, although hypersonic airliners would not have to go into full orbit. These could be called semi-spacecraft, but passengers would fly high enough to be called "space travelers." Technically such airliners will be possible, but it will be very difficult to make them affordable.

## HIGH SPEED TRANSPORTATION
This Boeing idea for a High-Speed Civil Transport plane (HSCT) has seats for three times as many passengers as Concorde and would fly 25 percent faster.

## ANTIPODAL ROCKET
Before World War II, German scientists were working on a project called the "Antipodal Bomber," a rocket that could travel to the opposite side of the globe. They imagined a rocket plane skipping along on the lower atmosphere at speeds of up to 13,500 mph (21,725 km/h). The project was abandoned in 1942.

# SPACE PROBES

**S**pace probes are silent explorers. Some are trying to discover more about the planets in the solar system. Others are on their way farther out in our galaxy and possibly beyond.

Probes are robots, about the size of a car, that are used to study other planets because the time and distance involved have made human flight impossible. Probes travel to their target, which can be a planet, moon, comet, or asteroid, and use equipment to gather information. Some probes travel unbelievable distances. In a couple thousand years, Voyager 1 will be closer to the Sun than to any other star. It will reach the end of our galaxy five billion years after the Sun has burned itself out and the Earth has ceased to exist. Then there are still countless more galaxies for Voyager to journey through. In billions of years, perhaps somebody or something will find Earth's space probes. Or will we discover a probe with signs of life from somewhere out there in the big black eternity one day?

## VOYAGER 1

Voyager 1 is one of four space probes on its way out of the solar system at more than 31,070 mph (50,000 km/h). It has been used to study the outer planets, including Jupiter and Saturn. In case it is found, Voyager 1 contains information about life on Earth with greetings in 55 different languages.

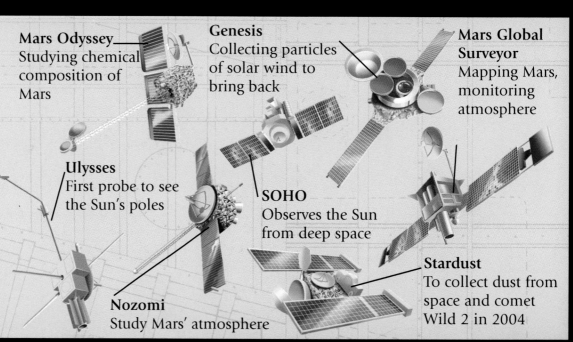

## PROBES GALORE

Several countries have built probes to explore space by flying past, orbiting, or landing on targets. Nozomi is Japanese, and Ulysses is a joint U.S. and European project. The U.S. Stardust is a space vacuum cleaner, the first probe that will venture farther out than the Moon and return to Earth with samples of space dust.

**Mars Odyssey**
Studying chemical composition of Mars

**Genesis**
Collecting particles of solar wind to bring back

**Mars Global Surveyor**
Mapping Mars, monitoring atmosphere

**Ulysses**
First probe to see the Sun's poles

**SOHO**
Observes the Sun from deep space

**Nozomi**
Study Mars' atmosphere

**Stardust**
To collect dust from space and comet Wild 2 in 2004

## CASSINI/HUYGENS

The Cassini probe was launched on a voyage to Saturn in 1997. It is the best equipped space probe ever built and will reach Saturn in 2004. There it will launch the Huygens probe that will descend by parachute down to Saturn's moon, Titan. Titan is the second largest moon in the solar system and may have an environment similar to Earth before oxygen became part of our atmosphere.

## SOLAR SAILORS

The sun emits a stream of tiny particles called the solar wind. The particles produce a light pressure when they hit an object. The power from solar wind is very weak, and in space there is nothing to slow down a vehicle. Future space probes may have huge solar sails so they can gradually accelerate to much higher speeds than those possible with rockets.

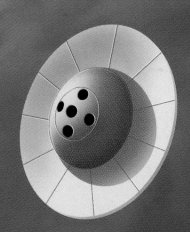

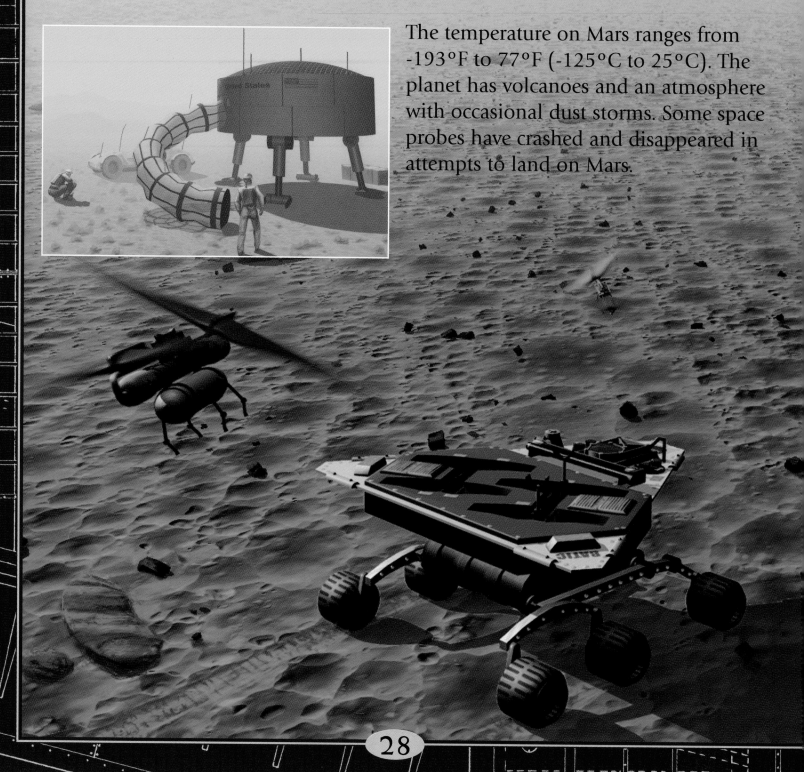

**PEOPLE ON MARS**
There is not much doubt that people could go to Mars or establish a space station on the Moon, but will the countries on Earth pay the huge costs of such an operation? On the other hand, can we resist the temptation to explore?

# MARS EXPLORATION

Is there life on Mars? As the planet with the most similarities to Earth, many people have wondered about this question. Martians have been imagined as everything from strange bacteria to vicious monsters.

The temperature on Mars ranges from -193°F to 77°F (-125°C to 25°C). The planet has volcanoes and an atmosphere with occasional dust storms. Some space probes have crashed and disappeared in attempts to land on Mars.

Others have made successful landings. In 1997, the Mars Pathfinder landed and released a little rover vehicle, the Sojourner, to explore the planet and send back images. In the future, robotic insect-like flying machines may help us learn more about this planet. People today do not expect to find monsters, but some hope we will one day land on Mars ourselves. The journey to Mars would take months, but NASA is conducting research into the creation of self-supporting habitats that would work on the Moon and Mars.

## SOJOURNER

The six wheel drive cross-country Mars rover is 24.5 inches (63 cm) long and 18.7 inches (48 cm) wide. Energy for its engine is supplied by solar panels. The rover has a top speed of under one mile per hour (1 km/h). The name "Sojourner," meaning traveler, was chosen for the rover from among 3,500 suggestions sent by children all over the world including Canada, India, Israel, Japan, Mexico, and Russia. The Pathfinder parachuted down to the surface from the Global Surveyor spacecraft. It was protected by a covering of several balloons (above), which softened its landing by allowing it to bounce. Finally the balloons were deflated and Pathfinder unfolded to release the Sojourner rover (below).

## ROBOTIC INSECT FLIERS

Future explorations of Mars could be conducted by small flying robots. They would be launched from a roving refueling base (shown left), which would move across the planet. This way, far greater areas of the planet could be explored.

## MARTIAN FLYER

It was once hoped that an aircraft would fly in the thin atmosphere on Mars in 2003 to mark the 100th anniversary of powered flight. This did not happen, but plans to fly on Mars are going ahead. Experiments with robotic, insect-like aircraft, which could fly well in the thin atmosphere on Mars, are underway.

# SPOTTERS' GUIDE

**R**ockets fly without the lift generated by the wings of an aircraft. To overcome the pull of gravity, great engine power and an enormous amount of fuel are needed. The Saturn V rocket contained 5.6 million pounds (2.3 million kg) of fuel! For each pound (0.5 kg) of spacecraft it lifted from Earth it burned up 50 pounds (22.7 kg) of fuel.

## SATURN V/ APOLLO
**Height:** 362 ft 10 in (110.6 m)
**Payload:** Apollo moon landers
**Launch date:** 1969

## D-1 (SL-13)
**Height:** 188 ft 8 in (57.5 m)
**Payload:** Salyut space stations
**Launch date:** 1966

## A-2 (SL-4)
**Height:** 142 ft 5 in (43.4 m)
**Payload:** Soyuz spacecraft
**Launch date:** 1967

## A-1
**Height:** 126 ft 7 in (38.4 m)
**Payload:** Yuri Gagarin in Vostok
**Launch date:** 1961

## A (SL-1)
**Height:** 95 ft 9 in (29.2 m)
**Payload:** Sputnik satellite
**Launch date:** 1957

## MERCURY-ATLAS
**Height:** 95 ft 2 in (29 m)
**Payload:** John Glenn in Mercury capsule
**Launch date:** 1962

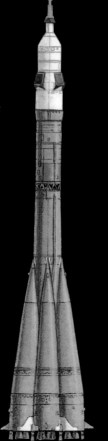

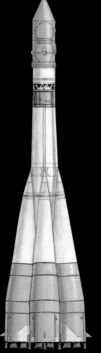

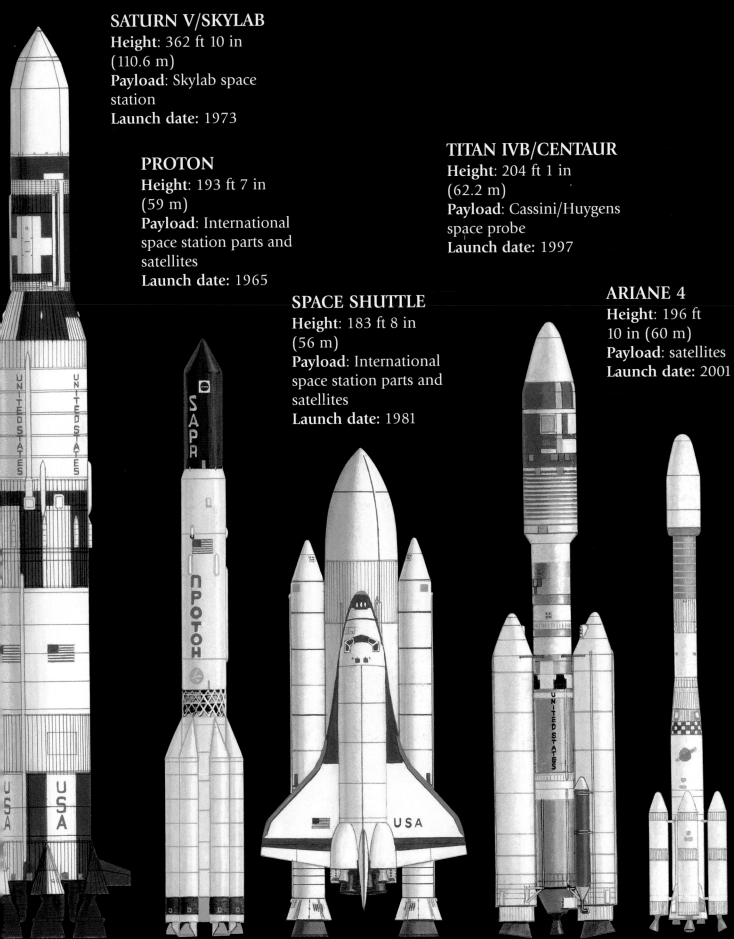

**SATURN V/SKYLAB**
**Height**: 362 ft 10 in
(110.6 m)
**Payload**: Skylab space
station
**Launch date**: 1973

**PROTON**
**Height**: 193 ft 7 in
(59 m)
**Payload**: International
space station parts and
satellites
**Launch date**: 1965

**TITAN IVB/CENTAUR**
**Height**: 204 ft 1 in
(62.2 m)
**Payload**: Cassini/Huygens
space probe
**Launch date**: 1997

**SPACE SHUTTLE**
**Height**: 183 ft 8 in
(56 m)
**Payload**: International
space station parts and
satellites
**Launch date**: 1981

**ARIANE 4**
**Height**: 196 ft
10 in (60 m)
**Payload**: satellites
**Launch date**: 2001

# INDEX

Aldrin, Buzz 12, 13
Antipodal Bomber 25
A-1 8, 30
Apollo 10, 11, 12, 13,
  16, 21, 30, 31
Ariane 4 31
Armstrong, Neil 12, 13
A (SL-1) 30
A-2 (SL-4) 30

B-52 15
Boeing HSCT 25
Boeing 747 16, 22
Buran 19

Cassini/Huygens 27, 31
Challenger Orbiter 16
Collins, Michael 12, 13
Columbia 16

D-1 (SL-13) 30

Gagarin, Yuri 8, 30
Genesis 26
Glenn, John 9, 30
GLONASS 7
Goddard, Robert 5

Helios 1 7
Hubble space telescope
  17, 19

Intelsat Early Bird 7
Intelsat 7 7
ISS 19, 22–23, 31

Laika 8
Leonov, Lt. Col. Alexei
  A. 9
Lifting bodies 14–15
Lunar Rover 13
Lunokhod 1 10

Mars Global Surveyor
  26, 29
Mars Odyssey 26
Mercury-Atlas 9, 30
Meteosat 7
Mir 20–21

Nozomi 26

Pathfinder 29
Proton rocket 23, 31

Salyut 1 21
Salyut 3 21
Saturn V 10, 11, 21, 30,
  31
Shuttle Orbiter 17
Skylab 21, 31
SOHO 26
Sojourner rover 29
Soyuz 21, 30

Sputnik 6, 7, 8, 30
Stardust 26

Tereshkova, Valentina 8
Titan IVB/ Centaur 31
TOPEX-POSEIDEN 7

Ulysses 26

Verne, Jules 4
Vostok 1 8, 30
Vostok 6 8, 9
Voyager 1 26
V2 rocket 5

Wild 2 26

X-planes 14–15, 24

# GLOSSARY

**ASTRONOMER** A person who studies the stars, comets, planets, and galaxies.

**ATMOSPHERE** The layers of air that surround Earth.

**COLD WAR** A state of political tension and military rivalry that existed mainly between the United States and the Soviet Union from the end of World War II until the early 1990s.

**COSMONAUT** A Russian or Soviet astronaut.

**DENSITY** The measure of how closely parts are packed together.

**DRAG** The force that pulls back on an aircraft.

**GRAVITY** The natural force that causes objects to move toward the center of a planet, moon, or star.

**JETTISON** To discard something that is either unwanted or no longer necessary.

**LIFT** The force that raises an aircraft into the air.

**METEOR** A chunk of matter from outer space.

**METEOROLOGIST** A person who studies the weather and conditions in the atmosphere.

**PAYLOAD** The cargo of an aircraft or the explosive charge carried in the warhead of a missile.

**PRESSURIZE** To maintain normal air pressure in an enclosed place.

**RADIATION** Energy, such as light and heat, that is given off in waves or particles.

**RANGE** The distance an aircraft is capable of flying with the fuel it has.

**SOLAR PANELS** Strips that convert the Sun's energy into electricity.

**SOLAR WIND** The stream of particles given off by the Sun.

**SOVIET UNION** The Union of Soviet Socialist Republics, a group of countries that were under communist rule from 1922 to 1991.

**THRUSTERS** Small rocket engines used for maneuvering in space.

**WORLD WAR II** A war fought from 1939 to 1945 in which Great Britain, France, the Soviet Union, the United States and other allies defeated Germany, Italy, and Japan.

7/24    5    7/19